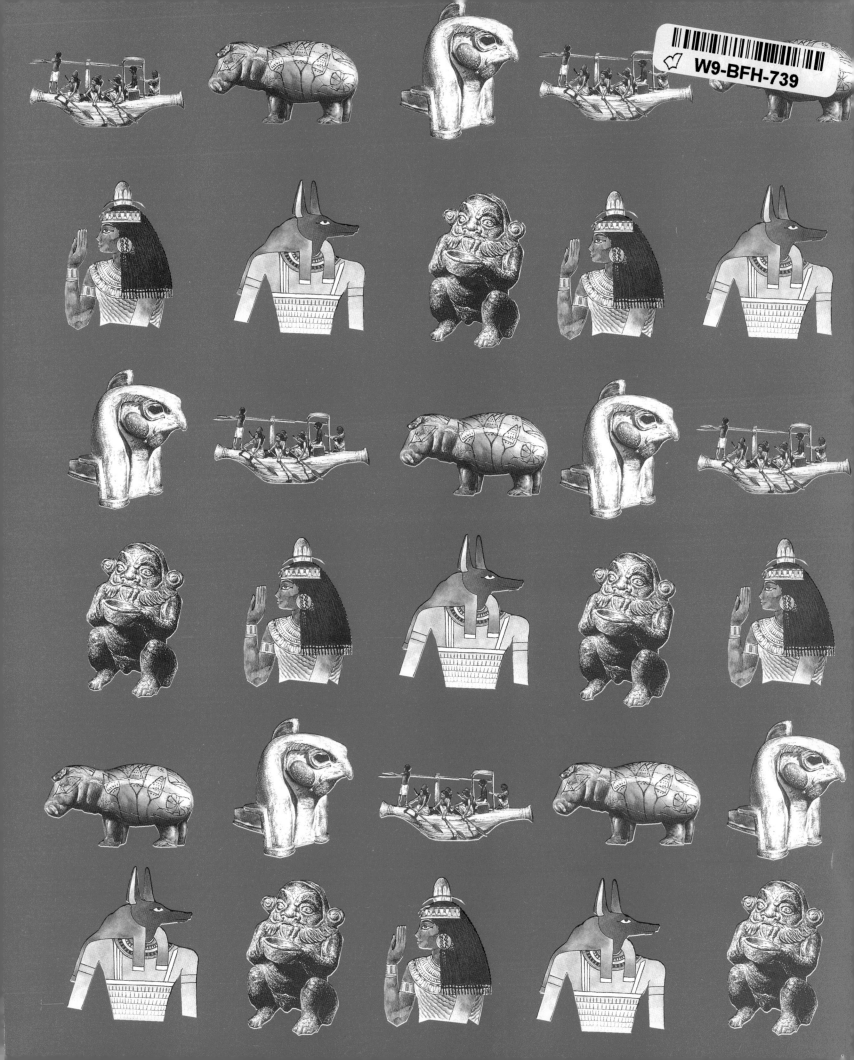

ANCIENT EGYPT

JUDITH
CROSHER

Viking

Acknowledgments

The publishers would like to thank George Hart of the British Museum
for his invaluable assistance and advice during the preparation of this book; Bill Le
Fever, who illustrated the see-through pages and jacket; and the organizations that
have given their permission to reproduce the following pictures:

Ronald Sheridan/Ancient Art and Architecture Collection:
13, 27, 37 (top left and bottom), 42 (top left), 44
Ashmolean Museum: 36, 38 (top)
British Museum: 7 (bottom), 14, 21, 22, 32, 37 (top right), 40 (top left), 44, 45
Peter Clayton: 40 (top right), 44
C. M. Dixon: 7 (top), 9 (bottom), 10, 30
Giraudon: 42 (bottom)
Michael Holford: 14 (bottom), 16, 19 (top and bottom), 23 (top left), 24, 26, 38 (bottom)
Museo Delle Antichita Egizie, Turin: 23 (top right), 42 (top right)
Ville de Montréal: 9 (top)
Werner Forman Archive: 6, 28

Illustrators:
Philip Hood: 4, 6, 8, 9, 10, 11, 12, 13, 15, 16, 19,
20-21, 22-23, 26-27, 29, 30-31, 32, 34 (Bottom left),
36, 39, 40, 43, 45 (Bottom)
Bill Le Fever: 17, 18, 25, 33, 34-35, 41
Richard Hook: 46-47
Kevin Maddison: 5, 45, (Top)

Editor: Julie Good
Series Designer: Nick Leggett
Picture Research: Ann Pestell and Jenny Faithful
Production: Linda Spillane

VIKING
Published by the Penguin Group
Penguin Books USA Inc., 375 Hudson Street, New York, New York 10014, U.S.A.
Penguin Books Ltd, 27 Wrights Lane, London W8 5TZ, England
Penguin Books Australia Ltd, Ringwood, Victoria, Australia
Penguin Books Canada Ltd, 10 Alcorn Avenue, Toronto, Ontario, Canada M4V 3B2
Penguin Books (N.Z.) Ltd, 182–190 Wairau Road, Auckland 10, New Zealand

Penguin Books Ltd, Registered Offices: Harmondsworth, Middlesex, England

First published in Great Britain in 1992 by Hamlyn Children's books.

First published in the United States of America in 1993 by Viking, a division of Penguin Books USA Inc.

1   3   5   7   9   10   8   6   4   2

CONTENTS

Without the River Nile the civilization of ancient Egypt would never have existed. It seldom rains in Egypt, and without the annual flooding of the Nile the land would be a desert. Every year on almost exactly the same date, July 15, the river would begin to rise — up to 30 feet at Aswan and less in the delta. By October it would spread gently over the flat land on either side, leaving only the dike banks and the villages on their little hills above the water.

Its [Egypt's] channels abound in fish and its lakes in birds. Its fields are green with herbage and its banks bear dates. Its tall granaries are overflowing with barley and wheat. Garlic, wheat, lettuces, and fruits are there for sustenance and wine surpassing honey. Her who dwells there is happy for there the humble are like the mighty elsewhere.

— Paibes —

As the wind blows from north to south, boats sailed upstream against the current and were rowed downstream toward the marshy delta. On long trips wealthy families took an extra small boat on which their meals were cooked.

THE BLACK LAND
The water of the River Nile was not as important as the thick layer of mud that it spread over the sandy fields, where the Egyptians grew all their food. This was called the Black Land; beyond was the Red Land, the stony desert. Every year the rise was measured on the stone columns along the river bank called nilometers: too much and the dikes and mudbrick houses would be swept away and the seed stores in the temples flooded, too little and the farthest fields would not be covered and there would be no way to grow enough wheat to feed everyone.

In the marshes people picked lotus flowers for making perfume, picked vegetables, and caught wild ducks for food. They gathered papyrus reeds from which they made boats, paper, sandals, rope, and baskets of all kinds.

TRANSPORTATION
As well as providing the soil for growing food, the Nile and its canals provided the main means of transportation. The river was always full of boats carrying families visiting friends, traders sailing between riverside towns or into the Mediterranean, and builders moving the great stone blocks and statues from the quarries to new temple sites. Many kinds of boats were used, from small ones made of papyrus to large boats made of wood.

Upper Egypt, where the grain was grown, was between one and 14 miles wide. Its symbol was a sedgeplant, and its deity the vulture-goddess. Lower Egypt's delta was 125 miles wide. Its symbol was a bee, and its deity the cobra goddess.

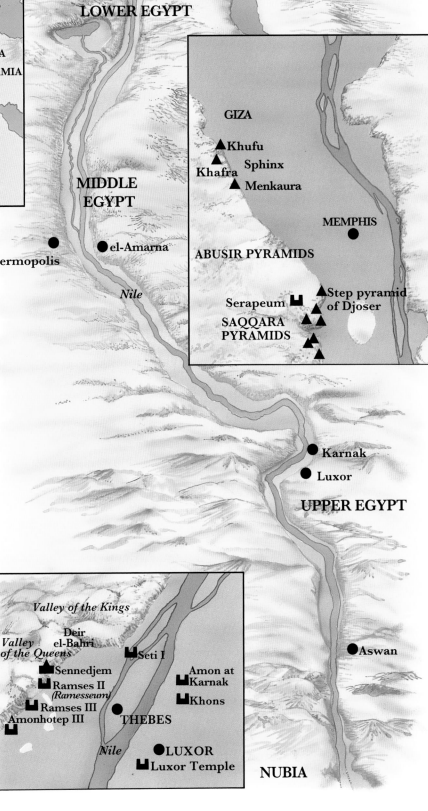

THE FIRST EGYPTIANS

About 5000 B.C., at least 2,000 years before the first kings of a united Egypt, wandering herdspeople were beginning to settle along the banks of the Nile. Protected by the desert on either side, they could live in peace. At first they harvested wild wheat, then as they settled into villages, some became farmers, growing wheat and barley and storing it in pits in the ground lined with rush matting. Some became full-time potters, some became hunters, organizers, and priests. People living in the delta traded with Syria and Mesopotamia and brought back the skills of copper-working, boat-building, and pictographic writing, which spread throughout the tribes along the Nile.

The beautiful objects they made show us that the Egyptians thought it was worth spending time to make things attractive as well as useful.

A UNITED KINGDOM

Gradually the villages began to cooperate, realizing that it was important to help each other in controlling the annual flood so that everyone could have a good harvest. At first, the 600 miles of country along the Nile were divided into two lands, Upper and Lower Egypt. Then, in around 3000 B.C. the two lands of Upper and Lower Egypt were united by the first king, Menes, and the first nation in history was created.

5

EGYPTIAN HISTORY

King Menes, sometimes called Narmer, wears the white crown of Upper Egypt, ceremonial royal beard, and bull's tail. The falcon-god, Horus, tramples 6 delta plants, each standing for 1,000 captives. Menes' servant carries his sandles.

The Egyptians believed that the world had been organized according to the wishes of the gods, and that it was their duty to ensure that things stayed the same. Dead kings were preserved in tombs so that their *ka* or spirit could benefit the country. Students copied essays written a thousand years before in an outdated style. Living pharaohs (as the kings of ancient Egypt were called) kept a connection with past kings by recording their own deeds in the same style. And the people's total dependence on the Nile's flood remained. Nevertheless many things did change.

DYNASTIES

In about 300 B.C. the priest Manetho wrote the first history of Egypt, dividing the list of kings into 30 dynasties consisting of a family or just a group of kings. It covers the years from about 3100 B.C. to 332 B.C.

It was King Menes of the 1st Dynasty who united the 42 nomes (provinces) of Upper and Lower Egypt in about 3000 B.C. He built a new capital city, Memphis. By then the calendar, writing, and accounting had been invented. Artists had laid down basic ways of working that were followed for nearly 3,000 years. Art was believed to have a magic power. Paintings and carvings in tombs and temples were a way of keeping the person, his actions, and his property alive, so it was important to continue doing things in the old traditional ways.

The chart on the right shows how the periods of ancient Egypt were split up, and the main time-scales involved. More information on this can be found in the Key Dates section at the back of the book (pages 46 to 47).

Early Dynastic Period 3100–2686 B.C.
Old Kingdom 2686–2160 B.C.
First Intermediate Period 2160–2040 B.C.
Middle Kingdom 2040–1786 B.C.
Second Intermediate Period 1786–1567 B.C.
New Kingdom 1567–1085 B.C.
Late Dynastic Period 1085–332 B.C.

Djoser's step pyramid is the earliest surviving large-scale stone building. He was high-priest of the sun god, and the pyramid was seen as a staircase up which he could climb to join the sun god's boat sailing across the sky.

THE OLD KINGDOM

Old Kingdom people believed that only the king could survive death, since he was thought to be a god. At first kings were buried in tombs like mudbrick palaces. However, in the 3rd Dynasty Imhotep, vizier to king Djoser, designed the first step pyramid by piling six stone tomb-shaped buildings, each smaller than the last, on top of each other. Later, during the 4th Dynasty, almost everyone in Egypt worked on the great smooth-sided stone pyramids and temples at Giza.

The 6th Dynasty in the Old Kingdom ended in a series of low flood seasons, which brought famine. The nomarchs or local governors returned from Memphis to their nomes to protect their people from starving invaders and to organize the distribution of grain. Instead of locating their burial tombs at Giza, they now built tombs in their own provinces, decorated by local craftsmen.

THE MIDDLE KINGDOM

In the 11th Dynasty, King Mentuhotep reunited the country. During this, the Middle Kingdom, the civil service became stronger, taking over control from the nomarchs. Trade was strengthened with Crete and Sinai, and the borders of Egypt were pushed south into Nubia and defended with massive mudbrick forts. At home people were becoming prosperous, and craft workshops were opened.

For people of the Old Kingdom the most important rules were respect for one's elders and for tradition. Middle Kingdom people valued fairness and justice more. They also believed that, thanks to Osiris (god of the Underworld), everyone could share the afterlife, and so they had themselves mummified if they could afford it.

At the end of the 12th Dynasty the central administration broke down. Subsequently, foreign rulers, called the Hyksos, took over Lower Egypt, bringing with them horse-drawn chariots, bronze, new weapons, the lyre, and the lute.

THE NEW KINGDOM

During the New Kingdom there were two very unusual pharaohs. Akhenaten tried to change everything, creating a new religion, a new art style, and a new capital city at el-Amarna. The other pharaoh was Queen Hatshepsut. The first woman pharaoh, she brought prosperity to Egypt in her twenty-year rule.

Kings, now called pharaohs (the word originally meant "palace"), were buried in rock-cut tombs in the Valley of the Kings.

For the first time pharaohs led their armies through the Near East, fighting to create and defend an empire. Captured city-states poured gifts into Egypt, and daughters of foreign princes joined the royal harem.

The New Kingdom came to an end just before 1000 B.C. Later, Nubians conquered Egypt but were driven out by the Assyrians a few years later, followed by the Persians, the Greeks, and finally the Romans.

Rahotep and his wife Nofret lived 4600 years ago, near the beginning of the Old Kingdom. These portrait statues of them, carved in stone and painted, were put in their tomb. Mustaches were very fashionable at that time.

This painting of picking and treading grapes and storing the wine tells us about Egyptian life. Notice the Syrian and Nubian slaves, conquered in battle, and the offering to the cobra goddess Renenutet in the center.

THE GOD-KING OF EGYPT

In other parts of the Near East kings ruled over small city-states. Only in Egypt was there one nation, and only in Egypt was the king thought of as a living god. While alive, he was Horus the falcon-headed sky-god, sitting on the magic Isis-throne. When he died, he became Osiris, god of the Underworld, and his heir became Horus.

Akhenaten and his family reward Ay (a faithful servant) and Teye (the royal wet nurse) by handing them collars from a public balcony of the palace. We have shown them wearing clothes, but the Egyptians would have shown all participants naked.

THE FIRST KING OF EGYPT

Re, the sun-god, was the mythical first king of Egypt, and every pharaoh was his son, born of a union between Re and the chief queen. His coronation took place both on earth and in heaven at New Year or when the Nile flood was about to begin, symbolizing the re-creation of Egypt.

In order to prove her right to the throne, Hatshepsut had this image of herself, wearing the war crown of Egypt and in the clothes of a man, being blessed by her "father," the god Amon-Re, carved on the wall of her temple.

THE PHARAOH'S LIFE

As a living god, the pharaoh was quite separate from the rest of the people. Everything he wore and used was designed for him alone and was consecrated at a special ceremony like the one carried out when a god was put in its shrine.

The pharaoh wore a bull's tail, which was thought to ensure vigor and reproduction. The king's major title was "Victorious/Mighty Bull." In ancient Egypt the pharaoh was thought to control the weather, and every year he performed the ceremony that was thought to bring the Nile flood. Every morning he carried out a ceremony in the temple, which was repeated by priests in every temple in the kingdom. It was as if he started the whole process of life each day. When he died, if his body was preserved, it was believed that his *ka* or spirit would remain in Egypt, spreading its power over the country.

THE POWER OF THE PHARAOH

Everything — and everyone — belonged to the pharaoh. The pharaoh alone could decide whether a person lived or died. Only the pharaoh had total control over the Egyptian people, because he represented the wishes of the gods.

A pharaoh could do anything he pleased. This partly explains the strange story of Akhenaten. In about 1350 B.C. he completely changed Egypt's religion. He announced that there was only one god; the Aten sun-disk. He abolished all the other gods, smashed their images, closed their temples, and used their wealth to build a new capital city at el-Amarna. Here he encouraged artists to develop new styles of painting and new ways of writing. No one opposed him because he was the pharaoh. When he died he was succeeded by Tutankhamon, who abandoned el-Amarna, returned to Thebes and Memphis, and brought back the old gods.

MARRIAGE

A pharaoh married several wives. The eldest son and daughter of his "Great Wife," the chief queen, were the royal heir and heiress. Because the god's blood ran in the pharaoh's veins, the heir and heiress would marry each other to keep it undiluted. If there was no heir, the royal heiress would marry the son of another of her father's wives.

A CHANGING ROLE

Although the pharaoh wore the same regalia and sat on the same throne throughout Egypt's history, his role did change. In the Old Kingdom he was most revered as a god, so much so that there is the story of the official called Ptahshepses, who was filled with joy because he was allowed to kiss a pharaoh's leg instead of the ground. During the Middle Kingdom, after the famine and civil war of the First Intermediate Period, the pharaoh was seen more as a protector, the "herdsman" of his flock. The New Kingdom pharaohs were admired as war leaders, great physical heroes. They were painted leading their armies.

This wooden statue of Tutankhamon as a baby, its gold earrings stolen, was found near the entrance to his tomb. His head rises from a lotus flower, like the sun-god who emerges from the lotus's opening petals.

The mummy of Ramses II inside this sarcophagus was nearly six feet tall. He was nearly 90 years old, balding with white hair, a long hooked nose, and very worn teeth. His hands and feet were dyed orange-red with henna.

9

MEDICINE AND THE LAW

Egyptian doctors, trained in the temple medical schools, were the best in the world, traveling all over the Near East to treat foreign royalty. Some were specialists, some surgeons, some general physicians.

PAYMENT

While royalty and wealthy families had their own doctors, anyone could consult the doctors in any temple's House of Life. For a private visit, doctors were paid in goods, like everyone else. A typical doctor's fee for a birth was a bronze jar, two pairs of sandals, some baskets, and a quart of oil.

TRAINING

Egyptian doctors studied real medical texts on papyrus, first written in about 3000 B.C. These papyri were divided into sections describing how to treat different injuries, listing medicines, and explaining how the heart worked. (They knew it circulated blood but thought air, water, nerves, and food went through it too.)

The textbooks stressed the importance of careful observation and gentle treatment, including rest and soothing herbal remedies. Egyptians had a great talent for observation and logical thought.

Doctors treated wounds with willow leaves, which contain salicylic acid (aspirin), to reduce inflammation, and copper and sodium salts to help dry up the wound. Cream and flour were mixed to make a cast for a broken limb.

Ma'at, daughter of the sun god Re, was goddess of truth and justice. Her image was placed on the top of weighing scales and was weighed in the balance against the dead person's soul when he or she came to judgment.

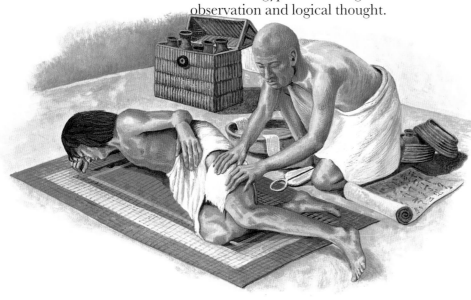

TREATMENT

An example of likely treatment in Egyptian times is the binding of a slice of raw meat over a stitched wound. The patient was probably told to remove the meat the following day and apply grease and honey to the wound.

An undigested mouse was found in the stomach of a mummified child. This shows another possible treatment. A child was made to swallow a dead mouse as a way of curing a bad cough.

With more difficult diseases, where they did not understand the cause, magic spells were mixed with the potions. Even if the medicine failed, the prayer probably was of some comfort to the patient.

JUSTICE

The word *Ma'at* originally meant level and ordered like a temple's foundation. Later it came to mean justice, truth, and righteousness. Justice depended on everyone being in his or her proper place and doing what he or she was supposed to. People felt that if they behaved properly they should be treated fairly. It was believed that Re created the world by putting Ma'at in the place of chaos. Gods and pharaohs lived by the rule of Ma'at, and judges were thought to be her priests.

THE LAW

Land was so valuable that there were constant arguments over boundaries. Anyone caught moving a boundary stone could have his ears cut off and be enslaved. The Treasury stored records of ownership and anyone could go and consult them. If a man was involved in a dispute about his land, he was able to look up documents going back hundreds of years. Because all land belonged in the end to the pharaoh, all landowners paid part of their harvest in taxes. Nonpayment meant being dragged in front of the magistrate to be beaten, questioned, and probably beaten again.

Criminals were either tried by the local magistrate or a group of local people like a workers' court. People spoke for themselves without a lawyer, and punishments were carried out straight away. Stealing hides was punished with "100 blows and five open cuts." More serious cases were sent to the vizier's court for sentencing. The vizier was the most important official and was in charge of justice and public works. Only the pharaoh had the power to pass the death sentence, given for perjury, treason, and murder. There was no written code, but decisions were recorded and could be looked up in the library.

The vizier was responsible for collection of taxes. Here a vizier measures the crops to decide how much tax the farmer, with his hand on the son's head, will have to pay.

In this painting from the tomb of the vizier Khentika, he judges district governors who have been caught cheating. On the right the wrongdoers are tied to a post and beaten. People could be punished on the spot for minor offences.

EGYPTIAN WOMEN

Of all the ancient countries of the Near East, Egypt was the one where women led the best lives, enjoying more freedom and rights than anywhere else. Greeks who visited Egypt were surprised to see that parents were as pleased at the birth of a girl as of a boy, and in many paintings you can see girls with their parents on the farm, in the garden of their house, or out fishing in the marshes as part of a family group.

RICH AND POOR

Of course in all countries women of very poor families helped in the fields, but usually among wealthier people women were kept shut away in their homes. In Egypt, however, they shopped and went to dinner parties with their husbands. Pharaohs would often boast that they made the country so peaceful that a woman could go safely wherever she pleased.

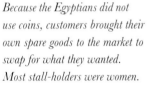

Because the Egyptians did not use coins, customers brought their own spare goods to the market to swap for what they wanted. Most stall-holders were women.

MARRIAGE

Marriage was a private, not religious, ceremony, and the most important part was the legal document that stated each partner's right to his or her own property. The new wife usually contributed one-third to a marriage settlement, her husband two-thirds. If either died the other could live on the income but could only give away his or her own share of it.

INDEPENDENCE

Having the right to own their own property and the right to work meant that few women were dependent on their husbands as happened in other countries. Women could seek work as midwives, singers or musicians, priestesses in the temple, and market traders. In fact, if her husband beat her, a woman could take him to court, and if he divorced her, he still had to support her. A husband and wife were often buried in the same tomb.

GODDESSES

One of the reasons why women enjoyed so much respect was the importance of goddesses. The goddess Isis was seen as the perfect wife. She spent years searching for the body of her husband, Osiris (the ruler of the dead), after his rival Seth had killed him. She finally avenged her husband's death through the use of magic.

Hathor, the goddess of birth and death was closely connected to Isis. She was the goddess who welcomed the dead into the afterworld, but was also, like Isis, believed to be the mother of Horus the falcon-headed sky-god. If a pharaoh was the living Horus, his chief queen, the "Great Wife," was also partly godlike and wore the head-dress of Hathor on her crown. Although the pharaoh might have many wives and children (Ramses II had 162 children), it was the son of the "Great Wife" who became the heir. If she had no sons, her daughter became heiress, and anyone who married her daughter became pharaoh.

A WOMAN RULES

Egyptian law even permitted a woman to become pharaoh. The story of Hatshepsut shows how. Her mother, Queen Ahmose, the "Great Wife," had no sons, so Hatshepsut married one of her father's sons by another wife and so made him pharaoh. Her husband was called Thutmose II. He died young, leaving her only a daughter. However, he did have a 10-year-old son by another wife. Hatshepsut became co-ruler with the boy. She should have let him take over when he grew up, but she decided that she liked power and had herself crowned pharaoh. She ruled Egypt on her own from 1473 to 1458 B.C. Her husband and father had been war leaders, but Hatshepsut concentrated on making her country prosperous, repairing temples, and organizing a great expedition to Punt, in northeast Africa, to bring back incense trees and other treasure for her "father," the god Amon.

A favorite way of spending a day out was to take the family fishing and hunting wildfowl in the marshes of the delta. A cat would be trained to collect birds that were stunned by the throwing stick.

This painting is of Hathor, goddess of music and motherhood, wearing the vulture headdress of Mut, queen of the gods. Over this are Hathor's disc and cow horns.

13

CHILDHOOD

The ancient Egyptians loved children, and the birth of a child was a joyful event, but also a dangerous one. If a family had a garden, they built a special pavilion of reeds where the mother gave birth, helped by her female relatives or perhaps a midwife. If they did not have a garden, the baby would be born in the house surrounded by flowers and paintings of the pavilion and of the household gods Bes (to drive away demons) and Thoueris (to comfort mothers in labor) on the walls. There were special prayers recited at each stage of the birth.

Egyptian children sometimes played with a paddle doll. This was a doll made of wood, with hair made of mud beads. Little girls' dolls were buried in their tombs with them.

Thoueris was a goddess, shown as a pregnant hippopotamus, thought to protect women during pregnancy and childbirth. She has the hind legs of a lioness and the tail of a crocodile.

PROTECTION

It was important to protect the baby as much as possible since many children died young. By casting the baby's horoscope the parents could find out which were its lucky and unlucky days and what it had to be especially careful about. To keep the baby safe, an amulet was hung round its neck. This could be a little Eye of Horus or a cylindrical case with a prayer on papyrus inside, usually a promise by the god to protect the child from colds, evil magic, or perhaps the dangers of travel.

Above are some of the toys young Egyptians played with: a glazed doll, a cat with movable jaws and teeth made of bronze, and balls made of palm fiber wound tight with flax string.

CLOTHING AND TOYS

Although paintings on tomb walls always show children naked, some children's clothes have been found. These are sleeveless tunics with extra sleeves, which could be sewn on in cold weather.

We know that children wore a long side-lock with either the rest of their head shaved or short hair because child mummies were found with these haircuts. Children were painted like tiny adults, but were shown naked and with their special haircut.

We can tell that children generally had happy childhoods — many tomb paintings show children with their parents, and it seems from these paintings that girls were as much loved as boys. There are also paintings of children with their pets: monkeys, dogs, pigeons, cats, and hoopoes (birds).

Their toys were simple: balls, whip tops, wooden dolls with string wigs and dressing up clothes, little wooden or clay models of animals, and wooden pins for playing skittles. Tip cat was a popular game played with a small oblong piece of wood called a cat, which was struck into the air by the player, trying to hit it over a large ring in the ground.

**You shall not spare
your body when you are young;
food comes about by the hands,
provision by the feet.**

New Kingdom proverb

SCHOOL AND WORK

A few boys went to school at the local temple. These were mostly sons of officials, but we know that poor children did go, perhaps helped by a local landowner. It must have been expensive: school lasted for about 10 years, and even if the teaching was free, the boy was not earning his keep during that time. If they ran away from school, boys had wooden blocks tied to their ankles; even then some managed to climb over the walls and go into town.

Once they had finished at school they went on to specialize in a profession. Some boys probably left earlier and became professional letter-writers in their village. Most people, however, had no education.

We do not know how many girls learned to read and write. Some did — there are letters to prove it — and in the tomb of Kenamun there is a picture of a woman with a scribe's palette placed under her chair, rather than the usual cosmetics.

FAMILY BUSINESS

But there was always something to do in the country, where most people lived. Most children started helping their parents, at about five years old, by feeding animals, collecting fuel, running errands and looking after younger children. Later, the boy would begin to spend time in his father's workshop or on the farm, learning his trade. Or perhaps he would be apprenticed to another craftsman in the village.

Ancient Egyptian children enjoyed playing games outdoors, just as children do today. They liked to play a lot of physical games, but boys and girls tended to play in separate groups. Girls must have spent a lot of time looking after younger brothers and sisters. The only evidence we have for children's games are paintings and objects found in tombs.

This clay "soul-house" from a tomb shows what a peasant farmer's home looked like. Outside stairs lead to the flat roof, where the family slept in summer. In the courtyard are offerings of bread, meat, and vegetables for the deceased. These model houses were often put into tombs to provide the deceased with food and shelter in the afterworld.

When the Nile flooded each year the country looked like a great lake. Riverside towns and country villages built on higher ground became islands above the waters. Each year the floodwaters brought more silt down, raising the level of the riverbed and the fields over which they spread.

BUILDING METHODS

You would think that, in time, the fields would become as high as the islands, and the towns would flood. This didn't happen for one reason: Egyptian houses were built of sun-dried mud bricks, which didn't last very long. When they crumbled, people just flattened the soil and built on top, so year by year the villages and towns rose too.

NEXT-DOOR NEIGHBORS

Official documents tell us a little about how people lived. The town roll of Thebes proves that different professions didn't live separately, as they did in some countries. It lists 12 scribes, 9 coppersmiths, a doctor, fishermen, 49 priests, brewers, a goldsmith, sandalmakers, and incense-roasters all living next door to each other.

A MIDDLE-CLASS HOME

The inside of an Egyptian house, even that of a wealthy family, might seem quite bare to us, with no cozy sofas, wardrobes, dining tables, carpeting, bookcases, or mattresses on the beds. However, it was cool and airy, with whitewashed outside walls to reflect the sun and high, unglazed windows to keep out direct sunlight and catch the breeze. There were woven mats on the tiled floors and bright patterns on the walls.

Egyptians cared a great deal about cleanliness. The bathroom was tiled with stone to stop splashes from melting the mudbrick walls. The lavatory seat was set over a pot of sand with an extra sandbox by the side. A rich nobleman might have a separate massage room next door.

FOOD AND DRINK

In every household, great and small, the most important job of the cook was preparing the daily bread and beer, which formed the basic diet of the ordinary people. Wealthier people ate more meat and drank wine instead of beer, often made from grapevines in their gardens. The Egyptians had at least forty names for kinds of bread. It was baked plain in conical greased pottery molds or flattened into round or triangular shapes, mixed with milk and eggs or nuts and spices, and sweetened with honey or layered with date pulp.

Everyone's dream was to have a whitewashed villa in the countryside, shaded by trees and grapevines, with a pool for ornamental fish in the garden. The house and garden would be constantly busy with servants coming and going.

THE HOME

Village Houses

Ordinary houses always had the same plan. Inside the front door was an entrance area leading to the living room, which had a low platform along one side for eating and sleeping. Off this were one or two smaller rooms with the kitchen behind, sometimes roofed with branches to give shade but let out smoke. As the population grew, towns became more crowded with two- and three-story houses and narrow, winding lanes. As children grew up and married, they subdivided their parents' house, adding extra rooms so that one house turned into several.

Shrine of Thoueris

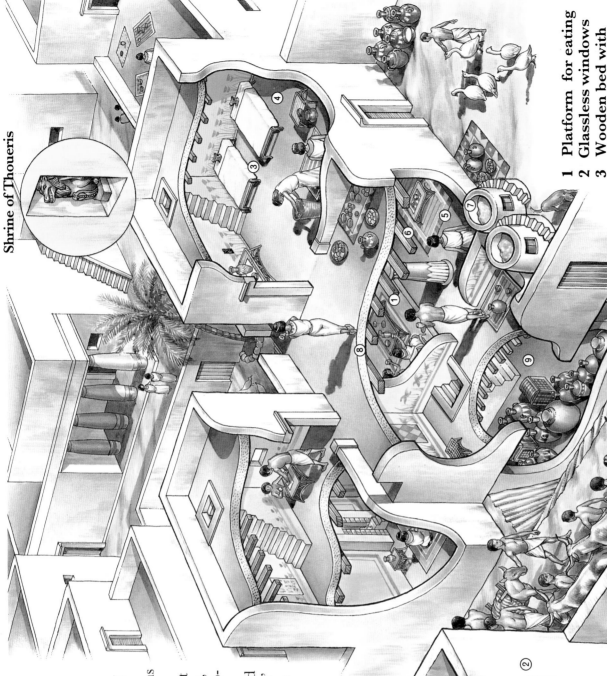

1 Platform for eating
2 Glassless windows
3 Wooden bed with plaited rush base
4 Portable lavatory
5 Main living room
6 Woven rush mats
7 Grain bins
8 Wooden beams supporting first story
9 Cellar for storage

WRITING AND CALCULATION

The Egyptians used a form of writing called hieroglyphics. This script is made up of about 750 signs, which include pictures of people, animals, plants, and objects. The last priests who wrote in this way died in about A.D. **400**, and the ability to read hieroglyphs died with them.

SOUND SIGNS

For years researchers believed that every sign actually stood for the thing it illustrated, but now we know it does not. For instance, the picture of an owl actually stands for the letter *M*. When writing first began in Egypt the picture did stand for what it described, for it was first used to record lists of items: a picture of the object followed by a number.

The Egyptians soon realized that this was not enough. A cow could be shown by a picture, but to write her name you needed more than this so, initially, 24 sound signs were invented. Because one sign for each sound made a very long sentence, they decided which groups of sounds occurred most often — *sh* was one — and invented a single sign for these sounds. This meant that there were hundreds of script signs. Lastly, because so many written words could mean more than one thing, they often put a picture of the thing being described at the end of the group of signs so there could be no mistake.

THE ROSETTA STONE

The Rosetta stone is a block of stone with the same information in three scripts: Greek, Demotic, and hieroglyphics. The last two scripts had been used to write the language of ancient Egypt. It was not until 1822 that a Frenchman named Champollion realized that some signs stood for sounds, and began to translate the hieroglyphs on the Rosetta stone, which had been discovered in 1799. Only then were the secrets of the hieroglyphs revealed to the world. Although we can now read hieroglyphs, we do not know how the vowels were pronounced since sound signs were only made up of consonants.

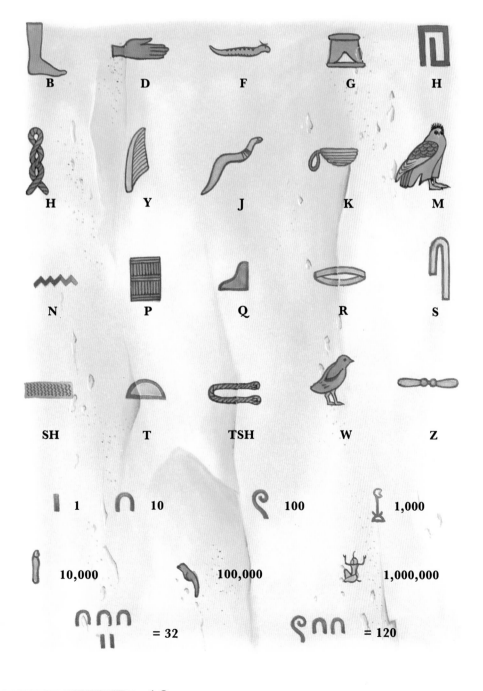

To the left is the basic Egyptian hieroglyphic alphabet. Hieroglyphs can be found on papyri, as well as on temple walls. Notice the variety of pictures used and the many references to nature.

FARMING AND CIVIL CALENDARS

The year was divided into 12 months, each with three ten-day weeks. There were four months in each of the three seasons and five holy festival days at the end of the year. This was the civil calendar. Because there was no leap year, it got more and more out of step with the farmer's calendar, which was based on the fact that at the same time every year, after being obscured by the sun for 70 days, the star Sothis (Sirius) reappeared. This was the start of the Nile flood. The two calendars only coincided once every 1,460 years.

TIME

An "hour" in ancient Egypt was longer or shorter at different times of the year. The Egyptians divided day and night into twelve equal segments, measuring from sunrise to sunset and sunset to sunrise, so a day hour was longer and a night hour was shorter in summer than in winter. Time was measured by filling a container called a water clock with water, which dripped at a constant rate from a hole at the base of the clock. Inside, circles corresponded to the water level as each hour passed. We are not sure whether the Egyptians were the first to invent water clocks, but this way of measuring time was used until mechanical clocks were invented in medieval Europe.

This is an Egyptian water clock. Water comes out faster when the jar is full, so if the hour dots are equally far apart, the jar needs to be wider at the top. As the length of an hour was different each month, there was a row of dots for each month of the year.

Thomas Young realized that some signs stood for letters of the alphabet and that rope-loops contained kings' names: "Ptolemy" and "Cleopatra." Using these clues, Champollion translated the Rosetta Stone.

Craftsmen used tools, such as this plumb level, to ensure that building surfaces were smooth and vertical. When the hanging bob just touched the lower wooden projection, the craftsman knew the surface was even.

HIEROGLYPHS

Hieroglyphs can be written left to right, right to left, or top to bottom. The clue is to start from the end the figures are facing. There were two other ways of writing. Scribes used hieratic, adapted from hieroglyphs, for quick handwriting. They did not rest their hand on the paper but held their reed pens vertically, like the Chinese. Demotic was a shorthand version used during the New Kingdom to represent ordinary Egyptian language in everyday documents.

USING NUMBERS

There were only seven signs for numbers, so writing 999 was a slow business. There was no zero and no multiplication or division. In order to multiply, the Egyptians added the number to itself as many times as they needed. They did use fractions but, for example, 3/4 had to be shown as 1/4 + 1/4 + 1/4.

ARTS AND CRAFTS

Painters, sculptors, and carpenters were all considered craftsmen in ancient Egypt, although there was not a separate word for artist. Each was a specialist, and it took several specialists to create a piece. To make a statue a quarryman was needed to cut the stone block, a sculptor to shape it, an inscriber to add the crucial hieroglyphs, a metalworker to insert the rock crystal and amethyst eyes, and a painter to finish it, for all statues were painted.

There was a great deal of noise and dirt in a craft workshop. The craftsmen were employed on a number of different crafts, such as making beds, statues, casks, and jewelry. The main metals used in these workshops were copper, gold, and bronze.

ARTISTS

The names of the artists whose works filled the tombs, temples, and palaces of ancient Egypt are almost all lost because they did not sign their names. We know one name by accident — in one tomb scene he painted himself decorating a statue. An admirer later copied the painting and added his name: Houy.

In tomb paintings craft workshops look clean and well-organized. In reality they must have been hot, noisy, and crowded with crucibles of copper or pots of glue smoking over charcoal fires, dust from grinding drills filling the air, and half-finished pieces passing from one worker to another. Most workshops were attached to temples or palaces, the craftsmen making pieces in their own time to sell privately.

JEWELRY

Everyone loved jewelry and wore as much as they could afford. Favorite stones were blue lapis lazuli, red carnelian, and greenish blue turquoise. A cheap substitute for lapis lazuli was made by firing copper ore and silica together to make rough glass, powdering it, sprinkling it into settings, and melting it to make shiny inlays. When this powder was mixed with natron (sodium carbonate) and painted on clay dishes or beads and fired, it was called faience.

Gold was mined in Nubia and the Eastern Desert, where conditions were so terrible that criminals sent there to work rarely returned. All gold was sent to the pharaoh's workshops because it all belonged to him to do with as he pleased.

20

In the most expensive tombs the pictures were first carved on the walls and then painted. Most, like Sennedjem's, were just painted. Some were not finished before a person was buried, and parts of the red squares can still be seen on the walls of excavated tombs.

TOMB PAINTINGS

Tombs were also decorated by teams of craftsmen. First the wall was smoothed and coated with gesso. Then a grid of squares was marked by holding a length of twine coated in red ochre taut against the wall and giving it a twang. The size of the squares was based on the hand of the main painted figure — his hand filled one square. The outline scribe then drew the figures following rules made in about 3000 B.C. Each part of the body fitted a certain number of squares. The whole figure was 18 squares high from the feet to the hairline. Arms were one square wide, eyes three-quarters of a square, legs from knees to feet were six.

Tomb paintings were thought to be partly magic. Things painted were believed to become real in the afterworld, so they had to be shown as clearly as possible. You can see the details of animals, fish, and trees best from the side, garden pools from above. Painters showed baskets and tables from the side, and piled the food up sideways into the air. Faces and legs faced the side, one eye, shoulders, and chests faced the front, and both big toes were put on the same side. In this way they could show all important features at the same time.

For carved walls, squares were marked and outlines drawn as for painting. On outside walls the artists carved the outlines deep into the stone so the sun could make strong shadows. Inside, they carved away the background. All carved walls were painted, but most paint has now worn away.

WOOD

Good quality wood from Lebanon was very expensive. Poor Egyptian-grown wood was made into statues, but they had to be coated with gesso, a mixture of chalk and glue, to make a smooth surface for painting. Wooden furniture was often painted or inlaid with slivers of ebony or ivory.

This is a blue faience (glazed pottery) statue of a hippo. The hippo was a common danger in ancient Egypt. It tipped over boats and trampled crops. There were two kinds of little hippo statues, one peaceful, one roaring. They were put into tombs, not in homes, and were there for the deceased to hunt in the afterlife.

THE MEANING OF COLOR

Paint was a mixture of glue and powdered minerals, which is why it has not faded. Each color had a meaning. Red (iron ore) meant evil, green (copper ore) resurrection, white (chalk) hope. Statues of the dead were painted black (lamp soot), meaning life in the afterworld, and the gods' flesh yellow (iron ore) to signify their golden skin.

21

FASHION

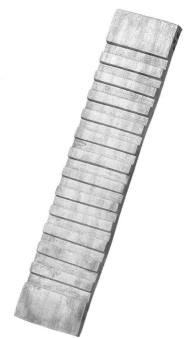

This board was used to make fine pleats in linen dresses. The damp linen was pressed into the grooves and allowed to dry. The best quality linen was so fine that it was almost transparent. Almost all clothing was made of linen.

A lady applies kohl (ground galena) mixed with water to her eyelids with a special stick. Kohl made her eyes look larger and protected them from disease. Her wig is of human hair coated with beeswax, and her mirror of polished bronze.

To find out what the Egyptians wore, we have to use as evidence the lists housewives made when they sent washing to the laundry, or the dead person's clothes, which were put into their tomb. Unfortunately, many of these clothes were thrown away by early explorers who thought the bundles of linen, sometimes grubby or half-rotted, were worthless.

DRESS

Luckily, when William Flinders Petrie, a well-respected Egyptologist, found a bundle of rags in a tomb in 1912, he realized it could be important. In it was probably the oldest dress in the world, still inside out. When the girl who wore it undressed, in about 2800 B.C., she didn't bother to turn it right side out again. This style of dress must have been popular in the Old Kingdom, as archaeologists have found several like it, some sleeveless.

The most common dress buried with Middle and New Kingdom women was a tunic made by folding a rectangle of cloth in half, sewing it up the sides, leaving holes for the arms, and cutting a keyhole for the head. Sleeves were made separately and sewn in when needed, usually in colder weather. These are the real clothes most Egyptian women wore, and they look very different from the tomb paintings, which often show women in skintight transparent dresses with no underclothes. In the New Kingdom women who could afford it wore over their shifts a large cloak of very fine pleated linen wound around the body, draped over the shoulders, and tied in front.

Children usually went naked when it was warm enough. When they reached about ten they wore the same kinds of tunics or kilts as their parents.

KHA

While workmen usually wore loincloths and short kilts, the architect Kha must have worn a loose shirt reaching to his knees over his loincloth for work; he had 26 shirts in his tomb. Many were carefully darned because clothes were so expensive.

JEWELRY

Jewelry served two purposes, as decoration and as protection. Most necklaces and bracelets have what were believed to be magic protective signs or amulets as part of their design.

All gold belonged to the pharaoh, so any gold jewelry would either have been given by him or made out of gold stolen from tombs. Ordinary people would have worn bracelets, earrings, and anklets of semiprecious beads strung on copper.

COSMETICS

Women painted their eyes with powdered grey galena (lead ore) and green copper oxide. Middle Kingdom fashion was for a grey line above and green line below the eye. They colored lips and cheeks with red ochre and hands with henna.

Ornate mirrors, applicators, and combs were designed to complement these cosmetics and were often decorated with objects from nature, including birds and flowers.

The architect Kha lived during the 18th Dynasty. All his clothes were put in his tomb. These are some of his 50 loincloths. He also had 26 shirts and 17 tunics. His wife's best cloak was found draped over her sarcophagus.

Egyptians loved brightly colored jewelry, and preferred semiprecious stones, glazed beads, and glass inlays. Men and women wore necklaces, rings, anklets, and bracelets. Earrings were not worn until the New Kingdom. This jewelry is fairly cheap, and was worn by ordinary women.

At parties and banquets women wore cones of scented ointment on their heads. As the evening wore on, the cones would melt, and a lovely perfume would fill the air.

LINEN

In Egypt's mostly hot weather, people needed light, loose, and easily washed clothes, especially as many of them did hard physical work. Linen was just right.

The flax, from which linen is made, was harvested at different times according to what it was to be used for. The young green stems made the finest cloth, "royal linen," which had 200 threads to the inch, or the next best, "fine thin cloth." The yellow older stems made good strong linen cloth for ordinary clothes, and the ripe, tough flax was made into ropes and matting. Vegetable dyes were used for coloring, but the Egyptians did not often weave patterned cloth because the colors tended to run in the hot climate of Egypt.

CREAMS AND SCENTED OILS

The Egyptians took great care in grooming since they thought it was uncivilized to be hairy, and they used scented oils and creams to keep their skins supple in the hot, dry climate of Egypt.

THE PALACE

Dancers at a banquet are shown in this detail from a wall painting from the tomb of Nebamun in Thebes.

This garden, painted on a tomb wall, shows how painters tried to show everything as clearly as possible. The fruit trees, date palms, ducks, and fish are painted from the side, and the pool from above so that you can see all the details.

I n about 1349 B.C., the pharaoh Akhenaten did away with all the gods of Egypt except Aten, the sun-disk. Only Aten and himself were then worshipped. He built a new city, which he called Akhetaten, "The Horizon of Aten," in which to live and worship his god. This new city was designed with wide streets and spacious, one-story houses, each surrounded by a garden. It looked very unlike other cities with their houses crowded together along narrow, twisting alleys.

Let song and music be made before thee. Cast behind thee all cares and mind thee of pleasure 'til cometh the day when we draw toward the land that loveth silence.

——— *Popular song* ———

PALACES

Near the temple Akhenaten built two palaces connected by a bridge. The official palace, of stone, contained the palace storerooms, harem, and huge reception rooms where he carried out his daily duties. The columns of the halls were inlaid with green, blue, and red glazes and gold. Statues in different colored stones stood against the painted walls. The floor was covered with wet plaster on which plants and birds were painted. As it dried, the colors were fixed in the plaster.

Over a central bridge lay the pharaoh's private palace. This was not very different from the houses of wealthy people in the city. Built of mud brick, it stood on a rise so that in the evening the family could sit out on the flat roof and watch the sun setting over the city. A gate in the high wall led into a flower- and tree-filled garden for family members to use during their leisure time.

WEALTH

There were no banks or money, so people were forced to store their wealth in their homes in the form of valuable goods for barter when they needed something new. Akhenaten's storerooms were filled with wine jars, grain and dried meats, ingots of precious metal, and alabaster jars.

PRIVATE ROOMS

The private rooms of the king and his wife consisted of an entrance room, living room, private chapel, dressing room, and bathroom. Across a small courtyard were the bedrooms of the six little princesses. Archaeologists think the larger room must have been a playroom. Its walls were streaked with paint as though children had wiped their paintbrushes there, and brushes and paintboxes were among the rubble when they excavated the palace.

The walls of the private rooms were decorated with pictures of the family playing together and views of the marshes with their wildlife.

KING'S PALACE

Palace Entertainment

Egyptians loved good food and company. Every large house had a living room like Akhenaten's in which to entertain friends. Guests were greeted at the door by servant girls offering garlands of flowers, lotus blooms, and cones of perfumed wax. During the evening these slowly melted and perfumed the air. There would be grilled meat, party bread, and fruit, all eaten with fingers, and lots of wine, plain or spiced and sweetened with honey. Early in the evening there might be storytellers or wrestlers to entertain the guests, with musicians and dancers performing later.

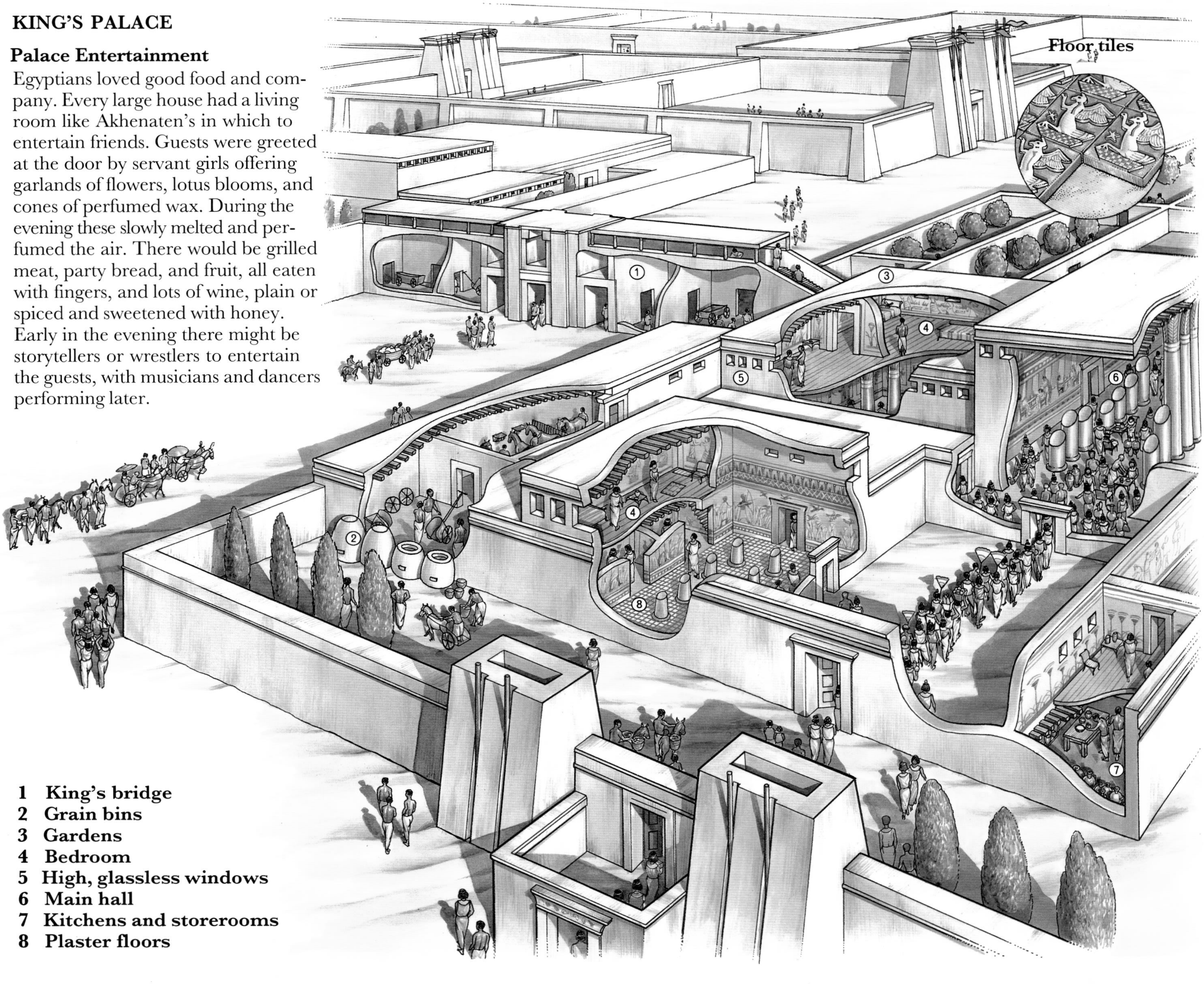

Floor tiles

1 King's bridge
2 Grain bins
3 Gardens
4 Bedroom
5 High, glassless windows
6 Main hall
7 Kitchens and storerooms
8 Plaster floors

PEASANT FARMERS

This wooden model from a 12th Dynasty tomb shows men storing grain in a granary while the owner's scribe records the amount. Models like these ensured that the dead person would have his farmworkers to help him in the afterworld.

Egyptian peasant farmers probably had a more comfortable life than farmers anywhere else in the ancient world. In the rich mud that the Nile flood spread every year over the sandy fields, the main crops, wheat, barley, and flax, grew quickly and easily.

RENTING AND BUYING LAND

All peasants were "King's servants" and bound to work on a particular estate, but they were able to rent or buy their own land and pass it on to their children. Even slaves — foreigners from Asia and other lands who had been sold into slavery or captured in war and worked on temple or private estates — could rent and cultivate land. They could be freed with a declaration by their owner in front of witnesses. Grants of land were also sometimes given by the pharaoh to retired soldiers.

Peasant farmers lived mostly in small villages built on mounds of high land safe from the floods, with a headman and council of elders to keep the peace.

TAXATION

The state officials arrived on the farm twice a year, once to estimate the crop and count everything from oxen and geese to bees, and once to collect the tax, which worked out as half of everything produced, paid in kind. This food formed part of the salary of the pharaoh's other workers. It was the farmers who were responsible for the wealth of Egypt for they produced enough food to support the rest of the population, enabling them to work as scribes, craftsmen, and priests.

IRRIGATION

In return for the taxes, the administrators organized the many tasks needed to control the flood. It was their good management that made the difference between starvation and having enough food to eat.

When the floodwaters began to sink, great lakes were left behind in natural basins, and it was then that the officials had to organize work parties to dig canals, build dikes, and mend sluices to contain and direct the water to where it was needed. In theory everyone except scribes, priests, and the elderly were called up, but probably some people paid others to take their place. Once this work was completed, the fields could be ploughed lightly so as not to disturb the sand underneath, the seed scattered, and herds of sheep driven over to tread it in. Even in the afterworld, this work had to be continued. Tombs always contained little model figures called shabtis, armed with hoes and picks, which acted as servants.

The workers cut the grain with flint-edged sickles and take it to the threshing floor for the oxen to tread. Then they toss it into the air with wooden scoops to separate the chaff, bag and count it, pay half to the tax man, and store the rest.

26

Without rain the land soon became hard and dry, so that all summer the farmer and his children watered it using buckets filled from the irrigation channels. In April the harvest began, and by the end of May the bare fields were quite dry, ready for the floods of late June.

A FARMER'S LIFE?

The quotation on the right is a description of a peasant farmer's life, written by a teacher to persuade his students that a scribe's job was by far the best.

However, records show that officials were not so hard on a farmer who had lost his crops through natural disasters, such as a hungry hippo visiting his land and trampling the crops, or a swarm of locusts.

He spends the day cutting tools, the night twisting ropes. His midday hour he spends working. The scribe moors at the river bank attended by Nubians with clubs. They say, "Produce barley!" but there is none and the farmer is beaten. He is ducked in a pool. His wife is tied up and his children are in shackles. His neighbors desert them. It is the end. There is no barley.

—————— Teacher ——————

One wall of the carpenter Sennedjem's tomb shows him and his wife (in party clothes!) ploughing and reaping in the afterworld, something they had never done in life.

When the farmers paid their taxes on everything they grew, they paid in honey, grain, oil, leather, or flax because there were no coins in Egypt until 380 B.C. These goods, which were collected by officials of the temples or the pharaoh, were used to pay almost everyone else in the land. Sailors, soldiers, priests, scribes, and craftsmen all worked for the pharaoh or for the temples.

The Prince of Punt and his wife Queen Eti receive the Egyptian trading mission sent by Queen Hatshepsut. The Egyptians brought necklaces of semi-precious stones to exchange for the valuable frankincense piled up here in a basket.

EVERYDAY TRADE

Because the same kinds of objects were usually swapped every day between the traders, people had a good idea of what things were worth. Everything had a value that could be stated in weights of copper or silver, but the metal itself did not actually change hands. Ten kite was the measure for one deben (about 3 ounces) and ten deben of copper was worth one kite of silver.

Sometimes the transaction was quite simple — a carpenter swapped an unpainted coffin with a scribe in exchange for a calf.

Sometimes it was more complicated. Records show the daily payment to the king's messenger to Seti I. This included bread, ox flesh, wine, sweet oil, olive oil, fat, honey, figs, fish, and vegetables.

Sailors on the merchant vessels traveling up and down the Nile were paid in grain. They came ashore every day to swap it for food and goods with the owners of little stalls set up on the docks. In the open-air markets people set up stalls selling everything from fish to cloth to cylinder-seals (for impressing a personal seal on, for example, parcels). The shoppers brought what they had, for instance a jar or a fan, and exchanged it for what they wanted.

SPECIALIST TRADERS

There were also merchants who traded in specialist goods. Khunanpu was a farmer living on the edge of the desert. He loaded his donkey for market and packed reeds, animal hides, salt, birds, and wood from his smallholding on the edge of the desert. He went to one of these merchants to swap his goods for things which he could not grow, like oil and bronze.

TRADE WITH FOREIGN LANDS

The pharaoh himself owned all the building stone, gold, copper, and turquoise in the land, and only he traded with foreign countries. The earliest record of trade dates from 3800 B.C.

Expeditions were sent to mines in Sinai for copper and turquoise, to foreign ports, to Palestine and down the Red Sea, possibly as far as Ethiopia. To reach the land of Punt in East Africa, it is thought that the Egyptians dismantled their ships and carried them across to the Red Sea, reassembling them on the coast to sail southeast. The pharaoh also controlled trade at borders, where caravans from Nubia brought skins, ostrich feathers, ivory, and ebony to exchange for beads and weapons.

Because of their belief that the pharaoh ruled everywhere that the sun shone, the Egyptians tended to show in their paintings everything that came from abroad as being a tribute to the god-king.

EDUCATION

A scribe's tools were a palette with two wells, one for black (carbon), the other for red paint (ochre), mixed with gum and dried; a water pot; pens made of reeds; and probably a little statue of Thoth, protector of scribes.

Writing was vitally important in ancient Egypt. The staff who looked after the army had to be able to read and write and to calculate. So did the architects who designed the temples and pyramids, the draftsmen and sculptors who painted and carved the inscriptions, the officials who collected the taxes and ran the pharaoh's estates, the doctors, lawyers, and magistrates.

EDUCATION

Schools are not mentioned in Old Kingdom texts but we know that even then princes were taught to read and write, and the sons of palace officials joined them for lessons. In the towns and villages boys might be sent to a local tutor.

In the Middle Kingdom there were "Houses of Instruction" at each temple and others probably connected with the treasury, the palace, and the army. These were probably not special buildings, just spaces in the temple or palace gardens where boys sat, cross-legged, on the ground around their masters. School was very hard work, especially during the first few years when the boys spent their time copying old-fashioned documents without understanding them. The Egyptians believed they should be beaten often.

After about 10 years of basic training in reading, writing, and arithmetic, the student began to train for a profession, which could be anything from a priest to an architect.

> A boy's ear is on his back: he listens when he is beaten. As for writing, it is more profitable to him who knows it than any other trade.

School copying exercises

People kept ducks and geese in pens, partly for eggs as there were no hens. They were fed on grain or sweetened bread pellets and roasted fresh or dried and salted. Here an official arrives to count the flock and collect tax.

30

SCRIBES

In almost every painting, whether it is of farmers in the country or craftsmen in their workshops, you will see an official with his pen and papyrus making notes. This is because everything in ancient Egypt was thought to belong to either the pharaoh or to one of the gods, so everything had to be accounted for. During the growing season an official from the palace or the temple came around to measure and assess the tax to be paid. In the workshops scribes noted the amount of paint or metal handed out. In the libraries records of the ownership of land going back generations were stored, and after every Nile flood the boundary stones were checked against these records.

Without the scribes and their careful records, Egypt as we know it could not have survived. A low Nile flood could mean disaster. The scribes had to calculate how much would be needed from the stores, how best to distribute it, and how much to collect in taxes the next year to make up for any losses.

During the Middle Kingdom those who ran the temples of the chief gods became wealthy landowners and employed not only priests but large numbers of scribes to oversee their libraries, workshops, farms, ships, and granaries. Like government leaders today, officials moved from one job to another: the ability to organize was the most important quality of a high official.

It was more likely for women from the upper classes to be educated than those of the lower classes. Evidence of this can be seen in tomb paintings that show palettes and scribal kit bags underneath their chairs. This artwork shows a painting from the tomb of Kenamun in the 18th Dynasty.

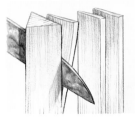

VIZIERS

At the top of the civil service (government) stood the two viziers of Upper and Lower Egypt. The vizier was the pharaoh's closest adviser, responsible for overseeing the assessment and collection of taxes. He was the chief judge in civil cases involving land or inheritance, and he was head of the civil service, responsible for the huge library of records, for the construction of dikes and management of the flood, and for receiving ambassadors and tribute from foreign countries. In his tomb, Rehmire, vizier to Thutmose III in the New Kingdom, wrote: "I was a noble, second to the king, praised at every moment." He quotes his pharaoh as saying: "The vizier is the mainstay of the whole land."

A papyrus-maker first peeled off the outer layer of the triangular stem. He sliced the pith into strips, laid them on a slab with more strips on top at right angles, and weighted it until the sap bonded the layers into sheets.

TOMBS

Shabti figures were put into the tomb of a dead person to do their work in the afterworld. Stories say the dead person would chant: "O Shabti. If I am called on to pull weeds or water the river banks or plough the fields, you will say, 'Here am I.'"

By carrying out rituals like the Opening of the Mouth, which Horus first performed for his father Osiris, the family helped the dead person travel safely and not become an evil spirit able to harm the living, especially children.

Without the body, the spirit could not survive. So the purpose of a great pyramid or a small tomb cut into the mountainside, like the one illustrated here, was the same — to protect the body of the dead person.

TOMB WORKERS

Sennedjem was an overseer who lived with his family in the village of Deir el-Medina. The village had been founded by King Amenhotep I during the New Kingdom for the workers on the royal tombs in the Valley of the Kings nearby, which is why it was in such a barren place, miles from water. The workers were paid in food and supplies from the temples of Thebes. Every day water was brought in by donkey; fresh fish, vegetables, and bread were delivered; and washermen came to collect the laundry to take to the river. The work in the tombs was passed down from father to son for nearly 500 years until it was abandoned in about 1080 B.C.

Everyone in the village was a craftsman, and these painters, carpenters, and stonemasons who decorated the pharaohs' tombs also made coffins and tombs of neighbors.

THE DEATH OF SENNEDJEM

When Sennedjem died he was mummified in a tent near the village. His mummy was brought back to his house to be put in its coffin. Family and friends pulled his coffin on a sledge to the chapel door, where they stood it upright on a little mound of sand, facing south. The priest said prayers, made an offering, often the foreleg of a calf, and decorated the coffin with a necklace of flowers. He moistened the lips of the coffin, made to look like its occupant, with milk, and touched an adze, a carpenter's carving tool, to the mouth, eyes, and ears. This was called the ceremony of Opening of the Mouth. These rituals were thought to help Sennedjem's spirit, his *ka*, return to his body. The same rituals were used for all burials.

He who reaches the other world without wrongdoing shall exist there like a god.

— *Montet* —

Then his coffin was taken into the burial chamber, and the priest performed a ritual to bring the painted figures on the walls to life with his adze. If an enemy got into the tomb, he would have to cut Sennedjem's name off the walls, paint over his face, and destroy the mummy in order to make sure his spirit died. This has been done in some tombs. The door was then locked, the tunnel filled with rubble, and Sennedjem was believed to have started on his journey to the Fields of Rushes, which were painted on his walls.

Just as the god in the temple of Thebes was offered food and drink every day to keep his *ka* alive, Sennedjem's family would bring offerings to his *ka* statue in the little chapel (right). Sennedjem was luckier than most of the pharaohs — almost all of their tombs were broken into and robbed, and the precious belongings that were buried with them were lost forever.

BURIAL TOMB

The Tomb of Sennedjem

The tomb of Sennedjem and his wife Iyneferty was found by Gaston Maspero, head of the Egyptian Antiquities Service in 1886. When he opened it everything was as it had been when they were buried at the beginning of the 19th Dynasty. In the tomb next door was their son Khons, who died before his parents. Iyneferty was seventy-five when she died, but her mummy case makes her look as young as she hoped to be again in the afterlife. She and Sennedjem are now separated — she is in an American museum, and he is in Cairo. On the tomb walls are paintings of food and equipment they might need in the afterlife as well as their portraits. Even if their mummies are destroyed, these and their statues make sure that their spirits will survive.

Sarcophagus

1 **Mudbrick pyramid**
2 **Limestone cap**
3 *Stele* (small carving and prayer)
4 **Statues of Sennedjem and wife**
5 **Anubis preparing the body**
6 **Sarcophagus of Sennedjem**
7 **Food and furniture**
8 **Shaft leading to locked door**
9 **Carpenter's tools**
10 **Painting of Sennedjem and wife**

THE PYRAMIDS

Between **2700 and 1640** B.C., more than eighty pyramids were built along the banks of the Nile. These consisted of one step pyramid and the later smooth-sided pyramids more familiar to us.

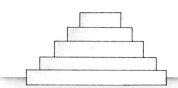

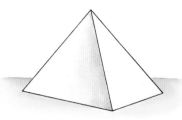

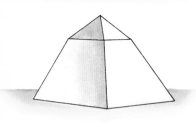

There are three main types of pyramids: the step pyramid, the bent pyramid (only one, built for King Sneferu), and the straight-sided pyramid, the more common type.

WHY BUILD A PYRAMID?

To the Egyptians of the Old Kingdom, their king was a living god. When he died he joined the immortal gods, but if they kept his body safe, his spirit would be able to return to it and his power would pre-serve Egypt. The pyramid was designed to keep the king's body safe forever.

CHOOSING A SHAPE

No one really knows why they chose the pyramid shape. It is true that it is a very stable, strong shape and so has a good chance of lasting a long time. It is also a sensible shape because the majority of the stone is in the bottom half: the further up you go the fewer stones you have to move. Some experts believe that it stands for the rays of the sun up which the king can climb to heaven. Others say that it is in the shape of the sacred ben-ben stone, the first part of earth believed to rise above the waters at the creation. You can see the same shape on top of obelisks.

When they were new, the pyramids were covered in smooth coats of polished white stone. Over the years this was re-moved to be used for other buildings, so the rough stone underneath was exposed. Middle Kingdom pyramids were built of mud bricks under the outer coat. When the outer coat was removed, they collapsed.

CHOOSING A SITE

First a site was chosen. It had to be on the west bank of the Nile, above the flood level and on a solid rock base.

The sides of a pyramid had to face ex-actly north and south. To do this without a compass the surveyor built a circular wall on the leveled site. At night he marked the place on the wall where a star rose in the sky. He then waited until the star set, and drew another line on the wall. The surveyor would then draw a line from both of his marks on the wall to the center of the circle. By bisecting this angle, he found true north.

THE BASE

Workers made a level base for the pyramid by cutting a channel around the site and partly filling it with water. The correct level could then be marked as shown by the water, and the water drained away. The channels would then be filled with rocks and pebbles to ensure that the base was completely even.

Finding true north for the site of a new pyramid involved working at night and plotting on a circular wall the place where a star rose and set in the sky.

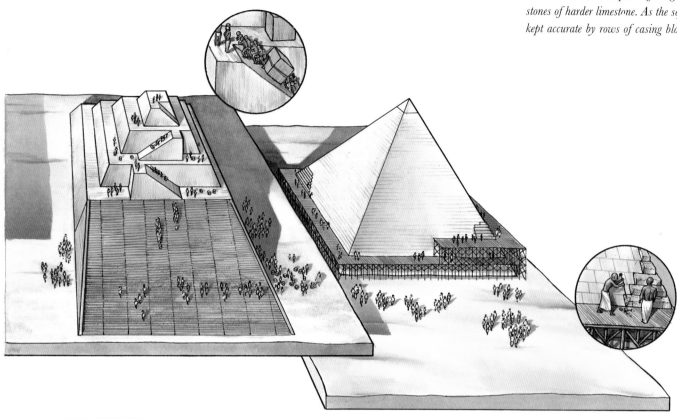

The main stages of building a pyramid. First, a level base was made using channels filled with water, then the sides were built one layer at a time, using ramps for each level. In each layer there was a middle square of rough stone, surrounded by casing stones of harder limestone. As the square grew outward, it was kept accurate by rows of casing blocks.

LIMESTONE

The inside of the pyramid was made of limestone quarried in Giza. The better quality limestone for the outside coating came from Tura, on the east bank.

Granite was too hard to be cut with copper tools as limestone was. Instead, balls of a hard rock called dolerite were used to bash holes for the insertion of small wedges.

THE INNER ROOM

The first stone blocks that arrived at the bank near the site were used to build the base of the causeway to make a firm road for the remainder of the stones. A room was constructed in the center of the pyramid to contain the sarcophagus (stone coffin). To put in the sarcophagus, workers filled the room with sand, dragged the sarcophagus to the top of the sand, and let the sand out gradually from the bottom. They had to do the same thing again to put on the roof.

Experts think that the pyramid was built one layer at a time, the ramp going up with each level.

Once the granite capstone was in place, workers began to remove the ramp, polishing the sides of the pyramid as they went. The last job was to cover over the causeway.

The burial chamber of the pyramid was carved with descriptions of the changes the king would go through until he became a god. On the walls of the burial chamber were false doors, openings to the outer world through which it was believed the king's spirit could pass. As a special favor the king might allow an official to build his own tomb near the pyramid.

THE TEMPLE

The pyramid was only part of the funeral site. The temple on the Nile bank was probably where the king was mummified. The roofed causeway, carved with scenes from the king's life, led to the temple at the foot of pyramid. This is where the priests made the daily offerings to feed the king's spirit.

Outside the core blocks there was a row of more carefully cut packing blocks, and the smooth white Tura limestone was used as the final coat. A granite capstone was put in place and the pyramid was complete.

GODS AND GODDESSES

Bes was a bandy-legged dwarf god with the ears, beard, and tail of a lion. He was much loved because he brought happiness to the home and protected it from evil. His image was often worn as an amulet.

The cat-goddess Bast (or Bastet), a kindly goddess, was connected with the sun, which protected Egypt. She was a goddess of joy, music, and dancing. Cats were treated as sacred in her honor.

There are many gods and goddesses to be found in the beliefs of ancient Egypt. These gods were often associated with individual nomes, or provinces, and their names and powers varied throughout the country.

CREATION STORIES

Most Egyptians believed that in the beginning there was only water. Then, just as happened after the Nile floods every year, the first mound of earth rose out of the waters of chaos. What you believed happened next depended on where you lived. People in Hermopolis believed that Thoth, their nome god, called forth the four frogs and snakes who made the great egg out of which came the sun, creator of all life. In Memphis it was the god Ptah who contained in himself all the other gods, and by the power of his thought and word created the world.

HOUSEHOLD GODS

An ordinary family living on their farm in one of the nomes would probably not know about all the gods. Most important in their daily lives would be the household demigods: Thoueris the hippopotamus and the little frog Hekat, who helped at childbirth; the seven Hathors who protected children; Renenutet, the cobra goddess of the harvest; and, most of all, the ugly dwarf Bes, who brought good luck to everyone. People painted images of these gods on their walls or wore them as good luck amulets.

THE NATIONAL GOD

In the Old Kingdom the pharaoh came from the nome of Heliopolis, which was protected by the sun-god Re. Like the pharaoh, the god Re was responsible for all Egypt. The nome gods often shared this national god's name and power. For example, the crocodile god Sobek is sometimes seen as Sobek-Re, and pictured wearing Re's sun-disk.

Horus, and his parents Osiris and Isis. Horus (left) is shown as a falcon-headed man, Osiris (center) is shown as a mummified king, wearing the white crown of Upper Egypt, Isis wears a sun-disk and horns.

THE NOME GODS

In the early days before Egypt became a nation, each of the small tribes that settled on the banks of the Nile had an animal as its protective totem, or powerful religious emblem. It might be a hawk, admired for its speed, or a crocodile to terrify the enemy. Each tribe also had its own hero, a legendary superman. They built the nome temple on the spot where he was believed to have been buried.

In time the hero/god and the totem animal became one powerful force. Few people could read, but if they put the totem animal's head on paintings of the god, it could be easily recognized.

On festival days the people went to their nome temple to take offerings and ask the advice or help of the god who was special to their province. These nome gods did not expect people to worship them regularly. When someone died their relatives took offerings of food to their tomb, believing that this kept the spirit, or *ka*, of the person alive and that they could hear and possibly help them. In the same way it was the job of the temple priests to feed, wash, clothe, and entertain the *ka* of the god so that its power would continue to benefit the nome.

THE STORY OF OSIRIS

Osiris (ruler of the dead) and his wife Isis (mistress of magic) once ruled Egypt. Osiris was a just and wise king, but his brother Seth was jealous of his power. Seth made a beautiful casket and invited everyone to a party. He promised to give the casket to whomever it fitted best. When Osiris climbed inside, Seth slammed it shut and threw it into the Nile. The casket floated to Byblos.

After years of searching, Isis found her husband's body, brought it back to Egypt, and hid it. Seth, while out hunting, found it in the marshes, tore it into fourteen pieces, and threw them into the Nile. Again Isis traveled through Egypt, searching for the pieces. When she found them all, she bandaged the body together, making the first mummy. Then she turned into a kite, her wings fanning life back into him. (You can see Isis's wings on some coffins.) By Osiris's spirit she had a son, Horus, who grew up to take revenge. During one of his battles with Seth, Horus lost his left eye. Thoth, god of wisdom, placed it on Osiris's heart, giving him insight into the afterlife, and Osiris became ruler of the underworld. Horus became king of Egypt. Because Osiris was the god of resurrection, he was also the god of spring, who enabled the dead seed to live again each year. This myth is one of many that are central to the beliefs of the ancient Egyptians.

Incense would have been burned in containers, such as the one above, as part of the ceremony in any temple.

Nut, the sky-goddess, arches over her twin brother Geb. His bent knees and elbows make the valleys and hills of Earth. Between Geb and Nut sails the sun-god's boat. At night, Nut's star-filled body descends to Geb, creating darkness.

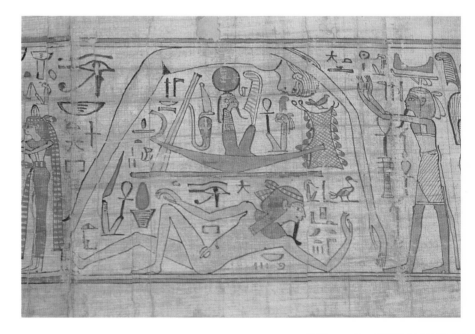

DEATH AND THE AFTERLIFE

These Middle Kingdom canopic jars contain the lungs, liver, stomach, and intestines.

The dead scribe Ani waits while Anubis weighs his heart in the scales against the feather of Ma'at. Thoth records the verdict and Ammut the Gobbler waits hungrily.

The ancient Egyptians believed that everyone had several parts: the *ka*, or spiritual double, created at birth and released from the body at death; the *ba*, or soul; and the *akh*, or supernatural power. As long as the body was preserved, the *ka* and *ba* would live. This is why it was thought to be so important to be properly mummified and laid in a tomb where offerings of food could be made, which would nourish the *ka*.

PREPARING THE MUMMY
In a tent called the "Beautiful House," near a temple, priests laid the body on a long, narrow table. The priest first pushed an instrument up the nostril and into the brain (thought to be worthless), and pulled it out in bits. Then he cleaned the mouth and filled it with sweet-oil-scented linen.

A priest in a mask of Anubis (the jackal-headed god of embalming) drew a line down the flank of the corpse, and a man came in, cut the incision, and was chased out with curses, for it was forbidden to injure an Egyptian. The priest removed the internal organs, putting back the precious heart, and filled the cavity with bags of natron (a drying mixture of salt, sodium bicarbonate, and sodium carbonate) and sweet-smelling gums. The body and the organs were covered with natron and left on a sloping table for 40 days, until they were completely dry.

The internal organs were placed in four containers called canopic jars, after being treated in the same way as the mummy and wrapped in linen. The stoppers of the jars were carved to represent four minor gods called the Sons of Horus. Imsety, the human-headed god, looked after the liver; Hapy, the ape-headed god, the lungs; Duamutef, the jackal-headed god, the stomach, and Qebehsenuef, the hawk-headed god, the intestines. The jars were placed in the tomb with the mummy.

The priests sewed up the incision, rubbed the body with cedar oil, and filled the eye sockets with onions or white painted stones. Finally, they put in stuffings of spices and linen to replace the internal organs of the body, and began to wrap it.

WRAPPING THE BODY
The body was wrapped with up to 150 yards of linen, sometimes old sheets, or special cloths given by the temple, once an old torn up sail. About 100 amulets (protective charms) were placed inside the bandages to strengthen different parts of the body. The most important were the heart scarab, which meant rebirth, the djed pillar for strength, and the eye of Horus for restoring health. Sprigs of rosemary and flower bulbs were also put inside the bandages, sometimes even pets. One girl had her pet monkey mummified and wrapped with her. An onion, for health, was put in the mummy's hand. At each stage prayers were said. Finally the mummy was painted with resin, a mask was put over its face, and it was put into a coffin painted with the person's portrait so that its *ka* would recognize it in the afterlife.

JUDGMENT TIME

Once in the tomb, it was believed that the *akh* began its journey to the hall of judgment. There it was judged against a list of 42 crimes. The god Anubis held the scales, the person's heart lay in one pan, in the other the feather of Ma'at, Goddess of Justice. The more crimes the dead person admitted to, the heavier the heart. If it outweighed the feather, then the Gobbler, a monster made of lion, crocodile, and hippo, swallowed it and it became an evil spirit, forever fighting the gods. If it passed the test it went with Osiris to live in the fields of Yalu, a place like Egypt though more beautiful.

MUMMIES

Only about 1,000 of the many thousands of mummies in Egypt are left. The word "mummy" comes from the Persian word "mummia," meaning bitumen, because the Persians wrongly thought the mummies were coated in bitumen (a tar-like substance), which was very valuable as it was supposed to cure everything. In the 13th century people began to unwrap mummies and send the bandages to Europe to soak the "bitumen" off. Then they decided that the whole mummy would be even better. Most drug stores had a jar filled with ground mummy to cure fractures and sprains and as an antidote against poison. This only became illegal in the 16th century. In the 19th century mummy wrappings were sent to America to make brown paper. This was only stopped when there was an outbreak of cholera at the factory. Today, mummies are usually preserved by Egyptologists and can often be seen by the public in museums.

If someone had lost a hand or foot, perhaps in war, a wooden dummy was made and wrapped with the body so the person could be whole in the afterlife. Wrapping took several days, which is known to us because of the beetle larvae found between the bandages.

39

TEMPLES

Khons, son of Amon and Mut, was a moon-god like Thoth. Like Amon, people could ask his advice when he paraded in his bark, and he would make the bark move or dip in answer.

Ramses II's temple at Abu Simbel runs 70 yards into the solid sandstone cliff. These are the 60-foot high statues of Ramses, his family in front of his legs.

The temple was the palace of the god, the home of the god's spirit, and the temple priests were the god's servants. Ordinary people never went inside the high brick wall around the temple buildings. The rituals that went on inside were believed to be vital to the spiritual life of Egypt, but the ordinary people of Egypt had no place there.

SHELTER FOR THE SPIRIT
Every community had its own temple dedicated to its own god, and every temple was virtually the same shape because it was believed to be a copy of the first temples ever built, thought to be designed by the gods. The temple was usually built on the spot where the god was supposed to dwell. The job of the temple and all the priests was to provide food and shelter for the *ka*, or spirit, of the god. In return the god was believed to look after Egypt.

At the Opet festival Amon-Re, chief god in the New Kingdom, was carried in his shrine on his sacred bark in a great procession from his temple in Thebes to visit his wife, Mut, at Luxor.

FESTIVALS
There were several festivals during the year where people could get closer to their god. Sometimes a statue of the god would be paraded around the temple walls carried in a closed shrine on a golden boat (the bark).

LIVING AND WORKING
In addition to priests, the temple employed scribes, librarians, doctors, teachers, kitchen staff, and craftspeople of all kinds. They were paid out of the food and goods produced on the temple farms.

Much of the land on which the temple was built and the farms were situated was left to the temple in the wills of ordinary people. In return the priests would make regular offerings of food at the person's tomb, or even allow a statue of the person to stand in the temple and share the god's food for a few days a year.

THE GOD AMON
During the New Kingdom Thebes was the capital city of Egypt, and its god, Amon (a creator and tribal god), became the main god of Egypt. Every time the pharaoh went to war, he asked Amon's advice. Winnings from military campaigns were donated by the pharaoh to Amon's temple at Karnak, and it became the richest in Egypt.

THE TEMPLE OF KHONS

1 Wall paintings
2 Priests carrying bark
3 Sacred pool
4 Store rooms for linen and oils
5 Sacred bark and shrine
6 Sanctuary
7 Library of sacred texts
8 Shaven priests of Khons

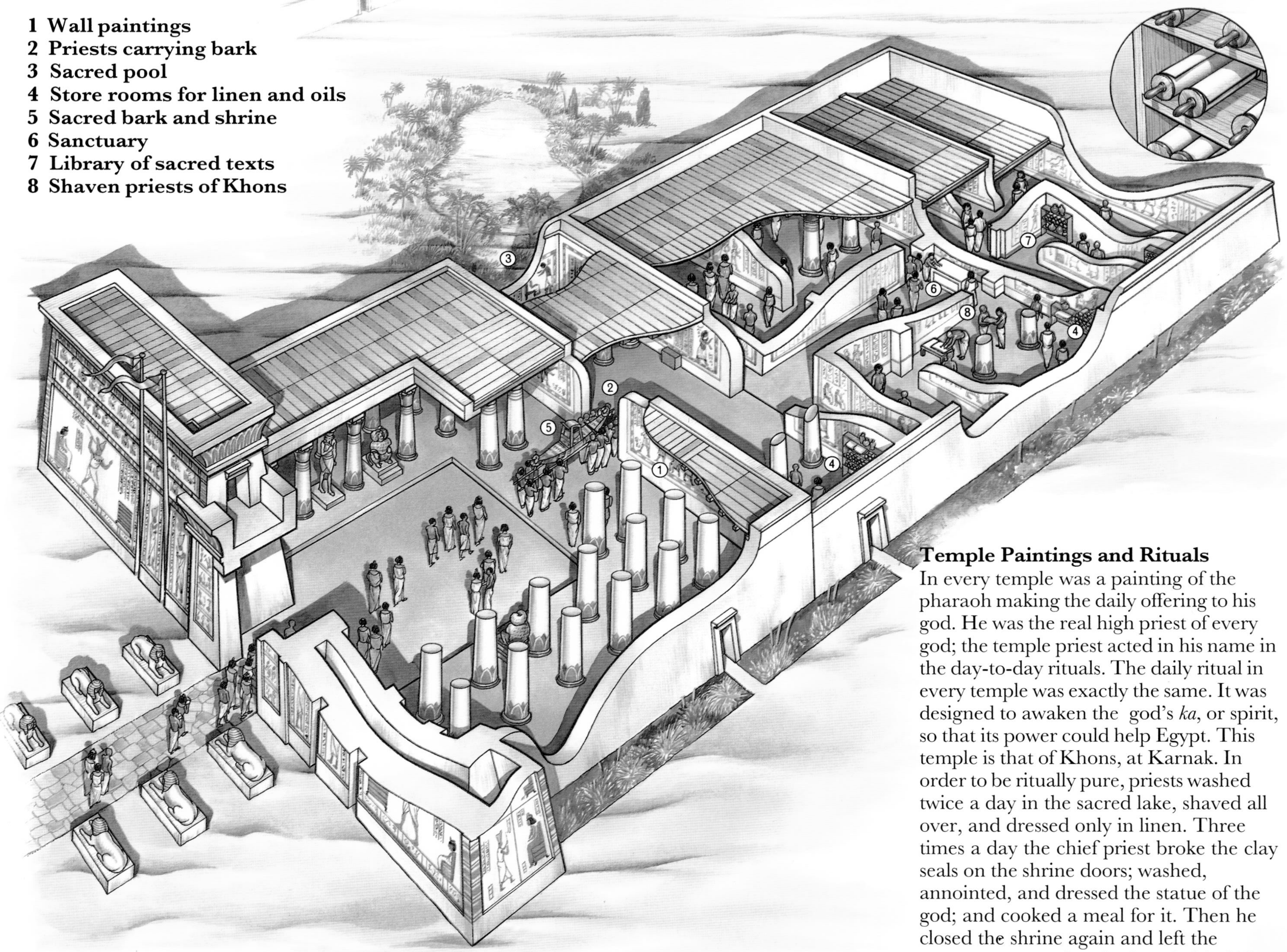

Sacred texts

Temple Paintings and Rituals

In every temple was a painting of the pharaoh making the daily offering to his god. He was the real high priest of every god; the temple priest acted in his name in the day-to-day rituals. The daily ritual in every temple was exactly the same. It was designed to awaken the god's *ka*, or spirit, so that its power could help Egypt. This temple is that of Khons, at Karnak. In order to be ritually pure, priests washed twice a day in the sacred lake, shaved all over, and dressed only in linen. Three times a day the chief priest broke the clay seals on the shrine doors; washed, anointed, and dressed the statue of the god; and cooked a meal for it. Then he closed the shrine again and left the sanctuary, sweeping the floor behind him.

THE EGYPTIANS AT WAR

The copper spearhead on the left dates from 1800 B.C., the harder bronze from 1300 B.C., and hardest of all, the iron spearhead, from 600 B.C.

When a battle was won, soldiers from the other side were recruited into the army. There would be Libyans, Hyksos, and Palestinians serving with Egyptians. These models are of infantry soldiers carrying shields and spears made of ox-hide.

It was after the end of the Middle Kingdom that Egypt had to take warfare seriously. For many years people had traveled along the caravan routes from Syria and Palestine to settle in the Nile delta. After a series of low floods and weak pharaohs, the country split in two. The foreigners, whom the Egyptians called Hyksos, took over Lower Egypt and made Avaris their capital.

THE EGYPTIAN ARMY

Against the Hyksos the Egyptian soldiers were hopelessly underequipped. They had no body armor, used heavy shields, small axes, and feeble bows that could only shoot about 200 yards, half as far as Hyksos bows. These weapons had been good enough during the Middle Kingdom, when the army pushed Egypt's southern border into Nubia and maintained it with massive mudbrick fortresses. Protected on the other sides by sea and desert, Egypt had never had to fight off an enemy before.

These paintings on the soles of a mummy's feet show a Nubian and a Syrian prisoner of war. Captives tied at the elbows like this appear on the soles of Tutankhamon's sandals.

It took a hundred years for the Egyptian kings of Thebes to equip and train their army. They had to learn from the Hyksos how to make and use the curved scimitar and new double-curved bow, body armor and, most important, the horse-drawn fighting chariot. The Hyksos had blocked the trade route to Lebanon, so the Egyptians built chariots from the only wood they had: doors and doorposts. Led by their king, citizens had to turn themselves into a professional army.

CONQUERING THE HYKSOS

Once they were conquered and Egypt was reunited, the Hyksos rulers left. Ordinary people stayed to join the Egyptian army.

To ensure the Hyksos were beaten, the army fought on through Palestine and Syria, conquering the small city-states the Hyksos had ruled. The Egyptians set up garrisons, invited the princes' sons to be brought up with Egyptian royal children, and welcomed their princesses to the harem.

A CAREER IN THE ARMY

During the 18th Dynasty the army was a good career for a young man. After his first period of training in barracks, he could go home until he was needed either for army service or public works, such as building temples. He shared in the booty when the army won a victory, and the pharaoh gave him a grant of land to retire on. A scribe could start as a pay-clerk and rise to scribe of recruits, in charge of organizing thousands of men.

Pharaoh Amosis had led the fight against the Hyksos, and from then on the pharaoh was commander-in-chief of the army, sometimes leading his men into battle and attending tournaments where champions from each regiment gave displays of stick-fighting and wrestling.

RULES OF BATTLE

The rules of battle were strict and respected by all the kings of the Ancient World. They agreed beforehand on the time and place of the battle. They always fought in daylight, their armies facing each other on open ground. Ambushes were not allowed. Each side waited until the other was quite ready before the trumpet signal to begin was given. The following account of the battle fought by Ramses III, however, showed that this battle had no rules.

In about 1200 B.C., plagues, earthquakes, and poor rainfall caused famine all over the Middle East. Trade failed and city-states started to break up. Bands of pirates armed with iron two-edged swords and sailing ships with battering ram prows swept through the Mediterranean. In 1190 B.C. a fleet of these pirates attacked Egypt. Ramses' ships, packed with soldiers, shadowed them into the river mouths of the delta. The skilled Egyptian oarsmen trapped the enemy ships against the shore where bowmen were waiting. Caught in the crossfire and having no oars the pirates were helpless and hand-to-hand fighting finished them off. As Ramses proudly inscribed on the wall of his palace: "We prepared a net for them."

In paintings and carvings in tombs and temples the pharaoh is always shown alone in his war chariot to make him look more impressive. In reality, he needed a charioteer to steer while he fought.

43

Pharos, the lighthouse of Alexandria, was built in 270 B.C. It collapsed a thousand years later — nobody knows why. Nothing now remains.

There were no strong pharaohs after the death of Ramses III in the 20th Dynasty. Once again the country became divided, and because there was no one to organize the distribution of food, it was the poor workers employed by the civil service who suffered most since they were considered last.

PEACE

After a period when there were two rulers, a family of Libyan princes seized power and for a time brought peace. This continued until they started fighting among themselves. The Nubians invaded from the south and ruled Egypt for 70 years.

DISRUPTION

Ancient Egypt was never independent again. As empires rose and fell in the ancient world, so each one conquered and then lost Egypt. The Nubian princes were driven out by the Assyrians, storming through Egypt with their well-organized armies and iron weapons. They appointed an Egyptian, Psammetichus, as governor. He encouraged traders from all over the world, Jews, Syrians, and Greeks, to settle in Egypt, and the country became prosperous again, exporting grain all over the world. This calm lasted for 150 years until the Persians conquered Assyria and took over Egypt. For nearly 200 years Egypt was part of their empire.

ALEXANDER'S CITY

In 331 B.C. the Macedonian Emperor Alexander the Great invaded Egypt, was crowned pharaoh by the priests of Amon, and founded a new capital city, Alexandria. He adopted some of the Egyptian customs, such as sacrificing to their gods. He never lived to see Alexandria become a great city. He died eight years later of fever in Babylon, aged 33. Legend has it that his body was embalmed in honey and taken to Alexandria to be buried.

Seven generations of Greek pharaohs, all called Ptolemy, ruled Egypt with their sister-wives, some called Cleopatra. The queen in the Shakespeare play "Antony and Cleopatra" was Cleopatra VII, who committed suicide in 30 B.C.

Artemidorus, a young Roman living in Egypt, died in the second century A.D., aged about twenty. The inscription on his mummy case says "Artemidoros Farewell." The lowest panel shows his winged ba *being reunited with his body.*

RULE OF THE PTOLEMIES

Alexander left Egypt under the control of one of his generals, Ptolemy Soter, and it was his family that ruled Egypt for 300 years, until the last of the Ptolemies, Cleopatra, committed suicide to avoid being taken prisoner by the Romans.

Under the Ptolemies Alexandria became the most famous center of learning in the ancient world. Aristotle, the Greek philosopher, left his library to Ptolemy Soter, and this was the start of the great library that in the end contained 400,000 books. Scientists, scholars, and philosophers from all over the Near East met to work there. Euclid developed his theories of geometry there, Manetho wrote the first history of Egypt, Hero invented the first steam engine, Erastothenes calculated the circumference of the earth, and there the Old Testament was first translated from Hebrew into Greek. In the harbor stood the lighthouse of Pharos, one of the seven wonders of the world, 500 feet high with a huge bonfire at the top which could be seen for about 70 miles.

Although the Ptolemies respected Egyptian traditions and their gods, life for the Egyptians was hard. Egypt was run for profit, with Greeks in all the best jobs and the ordinary people were treated as second-class citizens.

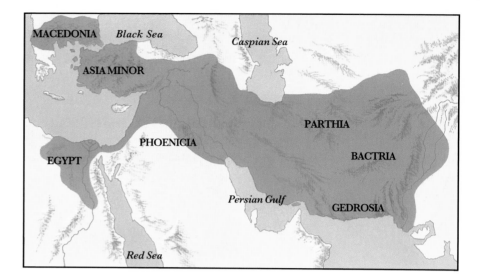

THE ROMANS AND CHRISTIANITY

If the Greeks were hard masters, the Romans, who took over power in 30 B.C., were even harder. They didn't live in Egypt, but left their agents to get as much profit as they could. It was at this time, with Rome as their rulers, that the Jewish community in Alexandria first heard the news of Christianity. By A.D. 200 there were several Christian communities in Egypt. They adopted the ankh (a cross with a loop at the top) as a Christian symbol, rather than as an Egyptian symbol for the soul, and used the ancient temples for worship. It was during this time that the culture of ancient Egypt finally died.

This map shows the empire of Alexander the Great. He defeated all the great nations he led his army against, including Egypt, and influenced their future development.

Early Christian communities adopted the ankh, a hieroglyph for "life," but before using the temples for worship, they destroyed as much as possible of the old religion, smashing statues and chiseling out carvings on walls.

Here we see Alexander the Great depicted as an Egyptian pharaoh. He is worshipping the god Amon-Re, whose son he was proclaimed to be when he first visited Egypt.

45

KEY DATES AND GLOSSARY

Early Dynastic Period 3100 – 2686 B.C.
(Dynasties 1st to 2nd)
King Menes (Narmer) the first Pharaoh
unites Upper and Lower Egypt and builds
his capital at Memphis.
Calendar and hieroglyphic writing invented.
First known textbook of surgery is written.
Irrigation and drainage projects begun.

Old Kingdom 2686 – 2160 B.C.
(Dynasties 3rd to 8th)
Imhotep designs the first pyramid, the step
pyramid at Saqqara.
Khufu (Cheops) builds the Great Pyramid
at Giza. Khefre and Menkaure build
their pyramids.
The city of Heliopolis and its god Re
become important.
Only the king is believed to enjoy eternal
life; only he and his nobles are embalmed.
Nomarchs become more powerful.

1st Intermediate Period 2160 – 2040 B.C.
(Dynasties 9th to 10th)
Breakdown of government. Nomarchs
return to their nomes. Chaos and famine
through the land.
Pyramids ransacked.
Tombs and statues destroyed.

Middle Kingdom 2040 – 1786 B.C.
(Dynasties 11th to 12th)
Pharaoh Mentuhotep reunites Egypt and
moves the capital to Thebes.
Powerful pharaohs reclaim power.
Amon of Thebes becomes an important god.
The first known schools are set up.
Art and literature develop, and many great
temples are built.
Osiris, god of the Underworld, is widely
worshipped.

2nd Intermediate Period 1786 – 1567 B.C.
(Dynasties 13th to 17th)
The Hyksos seize power.
New innovations brought by the Hyksos:
horsedrawn chariot, lyre, use of bronze,
improved spinning and weaving, and new
weapons.

New Kingdom 1567 – 1085 B.C.
(Dynasties 18th to 20th)
Pharaoh Ahmose defeats the Hyksos.
Many great pharaohs during this period:
Hatshepsut, the woman pharaoh, and
Akhenaten who tries to impose the worship
of one god and who builds a new capital
city at el-Amarna; Ramses II, who fights off
the Hittites; and Ramses III, who defeats
the invading Sea Peoples.

Late Dynastic Period 1085 – 332 B.C.

(Dynasties 21st to 30th)

Temple of Khons is completed.

Egypt ruled first by pharaohs of Libyan origin, then by Nubians.

Crafts flourish, especially metalwork. Nubian kings encourage study of the past and a return to the artistic standards of the Old Kingdom.

Assyrians invade. Egypt gains independence with help from Greece.

Persians invade and rule Egypt.

Greeks help Egypt to expel Persians, and an Egyptian pharaoh rules.

Ptolemaic Period 332 – 30 B.C.

Alexander the Great conquers Egypt and founds the capital city of Alexandria. Manetho writes the first history of Egypt. In 30 B.C. Egypt becomes a Roman colony.

Glossary

Akh: the soul of the dead person, which, after being judged, passes to the afterworld.

Amulet: a charm to ward off evil luck.

Ba bird: the personality that leaves the body at death in the form of a human-headed bird.

Black Land: the area of Egypt that was covered with Nile silt during the annual flood.

Canopic jars: four jars that held the liver, lungs, stomach, and intestines of the mummy.

Delta: the marshy land of Lower Egypt where the Nile splits into twelve main channels.

Demotic: shorthand version of hieroglyphs developed during the New Kingdom.

Dynasty: a group of pharaohs. Manetho, a priest, divided the lists of kings into 30 dynasties.

Field of Reeds: the afterworld, very like Egypt at its best.

Hieratic: a shortened form of hieroglyphs used by scribes for handwriting.

Hieroglyphs: a word first used by the ancient Greeks to describe the Egyptians' system of writing. It means "sacred writing" in Greek.

Ka: the double of a person, stored in his heart, which leaves the body at death.

Lower Egypt: the area of Egypt from the Mediterranean shore to the city of Memphis.

Mummy: the Persians called the wrapped bodies "moumia" which means bitumen, because they thought wrongly that the bodies were coated with this substance.

Natron: a mixture of salt, sodium carbonate, and sodium bicarbonate used for drying mummies before bandaging.

Nome: a province of Egypt. There were 42 nomes, each with a nomarch or governor.

Obelisk: a pillar carved into a pyramid shape at the top.

Red Land: the stony desert, ruled by Seth, brother of Osiris.

Shabti: a little model of a worker put in the tomb to do work in the afterworld.

Upper Egypt: the area from Memphis to the First Cataract in the Old Kingdom.

Vizier: the most important state official.